THE **FUTURE** OF **POWER**

HARNESSING
SOLAR
ENERGY

NANCY DICKMANN

PowerKiDS
press™

NEW YORK

Published in 2017 by
The Rosen Publishing Group, Inc.
29 East 21st Street, New York, NY 10010

Cataloging-in-Publication Data

Names: Dickmann, Nancy.
Title: Harnessing solar energy / Nancy Dickmann.
Description: New York : PowerKids Press, 2017. | Series: The future of power | Includes index.
Identifiers: ISBN 9781499432145 (pbk.) | ISBN 9781499432701 (library bound) |
   ISBN 9781508153320 (6 pack)
Subjects: LCSH: Solar energy--Juvenile literature.
Classification: LCC TJ810.D54 2017 | DDC 621.31'244--dc23

Copyright © 2017 The Rosen Publishing Group, Inc.

For Brown Bear Books Ltd:
Editor: Tim Harris
Editorial Director: Lindsey Lowe
Children's Publisher: Anne O'Daly
Design Manager: Keith Davis
Picture Manager: Sophie Mortimer

Picture Credits: t=top, c=center, b=bottom, l=left, r=right. Interior: 123rf: Alain Finger 12, Cris Kelly 21b;
Dreamstime: Julia Barlachenko 25; Historic Denver: Green Builing Advisor 14; NASA: Nick Glante 29; Public
Domain: Aliexpress/ kind South Africa 27; Building industry Council 17t, Eto Tam/NRM 13; Shutterstock: 22,
Vadim Sadovski 28; Thinkstock: Hemera 10, isockphoto 15, Stockbyte 5; Wikipedia: D. Bodine 17b, Andrew
Glaser 19, Globetrotter 21t, Haki Kimura/Kouhei Sagawa 7, Uffizi 8-9.

Manufactured in the United States of America

CPSIA Compliance Information: Batch #BW17PK: For Further Information contact Rosen Publishing, New York, New York at 1-800-237-9932

CONTENTS

SUN POWER

The Sun is a fixture in our sky, constant and unchanging. It is just one of the trillions of stars in the universe and—like any other star—an ongoing nuclear reaction in its core releases energy. Some of this energy ends up on Earth in the form of heat and light.

Life on Earth relies completely on energy from the Sun. Without it, we couldn't exist. The Sun's heat warms the planet, and its light allows plants to grow. In fact, nearly every source of energy on Earth ultimately comes from the Sun. Plants use sunlight to produce their own food from carbon dioxide and water. Humans and animals meet their energy needs by eating these plants, and carnivorous animals eat other animals.

FOSSIL FUELS

We also burn plants, such as trees, as fuel. The coal, oil, and gas that we burn in power stations are formed from the ancient remains of plants and animals. That is why they are called fossil fuels. Warmth from the Sun also creates wind. The Sun heats Earth's air unevenly, and the differences in temperature are what cause wind. Without the Sun's energy, the world would be a very different place!

A SUNSET OVER THE OCEAN. TO US, THE SUN APPEARS TO RISE AND SET EVERY DAY BECAUSE EARTH SPINS AS IT ORBITS THE SUN.

SOLAR POTENTIAL

In just 90 minutes, enough sunlight reaches Earth to meet the entire planet's energy needs for a whole year.

5

USING THE SUN

Over the centuries, we have discovered more direct ways of using the Sun's energy. For example, the Sun's rays can dry clothes hanging on a line, and many people in less-developed countries use solar ovens to cook their food. However, there are also more high-tech ways of using sunshine, and engineers are constantly working to refine these processes and develop new ones.

One of the biggest developments was the discovery of how to turn sunlight into electricity. This electricity can then be used to power appliances large and small—from pocket calculators to refrigerators. There are even solar-powered cars and airplanes. The Sun's heat can also be used, whether it is to heat water for homes or to generate electricity in large power stations.

CARBON-NEUTRAL HOMES

Architects are looking for ways to build homes that are carbon-neutral. This means that any carbon dioxide the homes release into the atmosphere—from heating or the use of electricity—is canceled out by clean energy that they produce themselves. Solar energy for heating and electricity is a key component of a carbon-neutral home.

THE TOKAI CHALLENGER IS POWERED BY
THE SUN. PANELS ON THE TOP OF THE CAR
CONVERT SUNLIGHT INTO ELECTRICITY.

FAST CAR
The Tokai Challenger
has a maximum speed
of 100 miles per hour
(160 km/h).

7

HOW DOES IT WORK?

The use of solar energy has a long history. In ancient times, houses in China, Greece, and elsewhere were designed to take advantage of the Sun's rays. The houses were built so that their main door faced south—the direction that received the most sunlight.

By about 1000 BC, the Chinese were using curved reflectors to focus sunlight on wood to light fires. Ancient historians wrote about a naval battle in 212 BC, during which the Greek scientist Archimedes used mirrors to focus sunlight on Roman warships and set them on fire. In 1767, a Swiss scientist invented the solar oven, using glass to trap heat.

PHOTOVOLTAIC EFFECT

The history of electricity produced by solar power began much later. In 1839, Edmond Becquerel

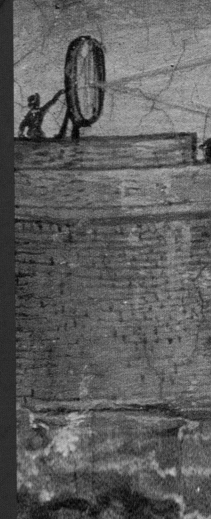

discovered that some materials produce an electrical voltage when struck by sunlight. This is called the photovoltaic effect, and it is the basis of how modern solar cells work. Later scientists conducted experiments to discover which materials were best to use. In 1876, professor William Grylls Adams and one of his students put two electrodes on a plate of the element selenium. They observed an electrical current when the plate was exposed to sunlight.

THIS PAINTING SHOWS ONE OF ARCHIMEDES' MIRRORS AS IT CONCENTRATES POWERFUL RAYS OF SUNLIGHT ONTO A ROMAN WARSHIP.

THIS LARGE SOLAR ENERGY INSTALLATION USES THE PHOTOVOLTAIC EFFECT TO CONVERT SUNLIGHT INTO ELECTRICITY.

10

ELECTRICITY FROM LIGHT

Solar cells based on William Grylls Adams' experiments were not very efficient—they were only able to convert 1–2 percent of the potential energy from the sunlight into electricity. Researchers kept working on the problem, and in 1954 the first practical photovoltaic solar cell was developed at Bell Laboratories. Its inventors were soon able to push its efficiency up to about 10 percent.

Modern solar cells use thin wafers made of a semiconductor material, such as silicon. The wafer has an electric field that is positive on one side and negative on the other. Conductors are attached to both the positive and negative sides of the wafer to form an electrical circuit. When sunlight hits the wafer, electrons from the silicon atoms are knocked loose. The loose electrons are then captured in the form of an electrical current. This electricity can be used to power a light, a calculator, or another device.

The first solar cells were expensive and inefficient, but scientists saw their potential, especially for powering spacecraft. Researchers at NASA and elsewhere improved the technology. Some modern solar panels operate at more than 20 percent efficiency.

SOLAR OVEN

The world's biggest solar oven is at Odeilo in France. Mirrors focus the Sun's rays on a small area to produce temperatures as high as 6,300°F (3,500°C).

SOLAR THERMAL ENERGY

Using a photovoltaic cell is not the only way to produce electricity from the Sun's energy. A system called concentrating solar power (CSP) uses the Sun's heat, rather than its light. In a CSP plant, the Sun's energy heats up a liquid such as oil to temperatures of 750°F (400°C) or more. This super-hot fluid is used to boil water to make steam. The steam turns a turbine to generate electricity, in the same way that coal-fired power plants work.

Some types of CSP stations use a tall central tower surrounded by mirrors. The mirrors move throughout the day to keep the moving Sun's rays focused on the central tower. There, they heat up a fluid that can be used to make steam and generate electricity.

CSP POWER

Ivanpah is the world's
biggest CSP facility, producing
370 megawatts of electricity.
Even bigger CSP power
stations are planned.

ONE OF THE TOWERS OF THE IVANPAH
CONCENTRATING SOLAR POWER STATION
IN THE MOJAVE DESERT, CALIFORNIA.

13

SOLAR WATER HEATING

We can also use solar energy to heat water for use in homes and businesses. About 18 percent of the energy used by an average household goes toward heating water for showers, washing machines, and dishwashers.

A solar water heating system consists of solar collectors on the roof and a storage tank. A solar collector is a flat, insulated box with glass on the top. Inside the box are thin tubes filled with a fluid that the Sun's heat then warms. The hot water produced is kept in the storage tank until it is needed. Solar water heating systems are often combined with a traditional water heater so that hot water is available at all times.

SOLAR HOUSE

In 1939, researchers at the Massachusetts Institute of Technology built the first "solar house." This experimental building used solar collectors on the roof to heat water. The water ran through thin tubes in the solar collectors and then down to a hot water tank in the basement. The hot water heated air to warm the house.

SOLAR ENERGY CAN BE USED TO
HEAT THE WATER USED IN SHOWERS.

15

HOW WE USE SOLAR ENERGY

Solar power stations supply electricity to the grid, and many homes use solar water heating, but we can also use solar energy in a range of other ways. It is especially useful for powering small, portable devices such as phones. In remote locations where there is nowhere to plug in a charger, being able to charge a phone using a small solar panel can be a lifesaver. Solar panels can provide electricity to medical clinics in places without a reliable supply of electricity from the grid.

Solar energy is also a good way of powering stationary devices. Many homes have outdoor lights with solar panels that charge during the day, letting the lights glow at night. Street lights, speed cameras, traffic lights, and emergency phone systems are sometimes powered by solar panels. They often have battery packs that store energy so that they can work both day and night.

Engineers have been working for decades on solar-powered transportation, such as cars and airplanes. Solar cars use photovoltaic cells to produce the electricity that powers the car. So far, the technology is not practical for most uses, since the cars travel at low speeds and have a limited range.

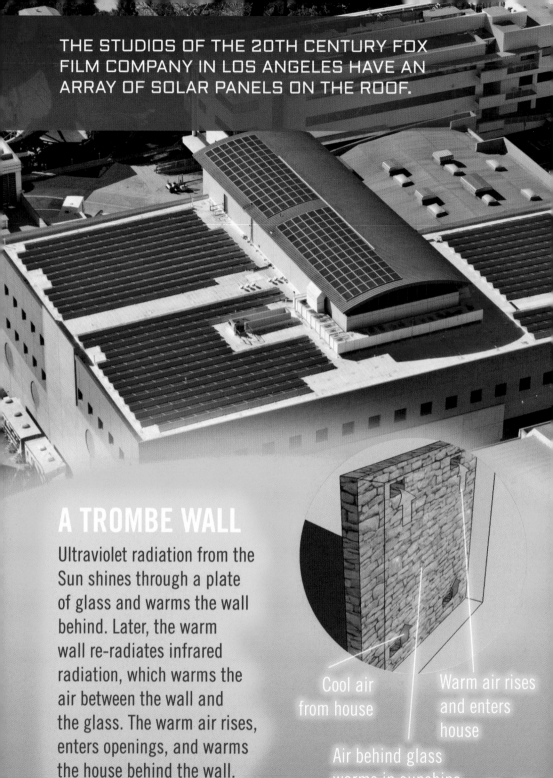

THE STUDIOS OF THE 20TH CENTURY FOX FILM COMPANY IN LOS ANGELES HAVE AN ARRAY OF SOLAR PANELS ON THE ROOF.

A TROMBE WALL

Ultraviolet radiation from the Sun shines through a plate of glass and warms the wall behind. Later, the warm wall re-radiates infrared radiation, which warms the air between the wall and the glass. The warm air rises, enters openings, and warms the house behind the wall.

Cool air from house

Warm air rises and enters house

Air behind glass warms in sunshine

17

GOOD AND BAD

Solar power has huge potential, so it's no wonder that governments and corporations are investing in it. One of its biggest advantages is that it is renewable. This means that the source of solar energy—the Sun—will always be there. Unlike fossil fuels such as oil, coal, or natural gas, it will never run out.

We are rapidly using up Earth's supplies of fossil fuels. We need to find other, more renewable, ways of powering our lives before fossils fuels run out. Solar energy is part of the solution.

HOW WE USE SOLAR ENERGY

Solar energy is a low-carbon form of power. Burning fossil fuels releases carbon dioxide into the atmosphere. When the carbon dioxide builds up, it traps the Sun's heat close to Earth, instead of letting it bounce back into space. Over time, this leads to an increase in the planet's average temperature, which could cause dangerous changes in the weather. Governments have signed international agreements to reduce their carbon emissions. Switching to cleaner forms of energy is one way to achieve this.

THE HELIOTROPE BUILDING IN GERMANY HAS SOLAR PANELS ON ITS ROOF. THE BUILDING ROTATES TO TRACK THE SUN'S MOVEMENT.

19

FLEXIBLE POWER

Solar power is more than just renewable and clean—it is also incredibly flexible. It can be used in large-scale settings, such as the giant electricity-generating stations that use photovoltaic or CSP technology. And it can also be used to power individual houses, or even single devices. The range of possible uses is enormous. And because the Sun shines on the entire planet, it can be used virtually anywhere, unlike geothermal or tidal power.

There are other renewable and clean ways of generating electricity, such as wind and wave power, but the Sun's energy can also be used for heating. By using the Sun's energy to heat water, homeowners can reduce their energy bills and reduce their "carbon footprint." Solar power can be used to run household heating systems, and it can even be used as part of a cooling system!

NOT EXPENSIVE

When setting up a solar power system, the costs are mainly up front. This means that producing and installing the equipment can be expensive. However, once the equipment is operating, the cost of producing the electricity or heat is very small. Most solar installations have low maintenance costs.

COOKING OVENS

In many parts of the world, people cook over wood-burning fires. Toxic smoke from these fires kills 1.5 million women and children every year. Lightweight solar ovens (right) produce no smoke and don't require forests to be cut down for wood.

21

THIS SOLAR ARRAY CAN'T PRODUCE ENERGY ON A DAY WHEN IT IS CLOUDY AND RAINING AND THERE IS NO SUNSHINE.

SOLAR PROBLEMS

Although it is abundant and clean, solar energy is far from perfect. The biggest problem is that the Sun only shines during the day. Even then, in many places clouds block the Sun out. The power grid needs a constant supply of electricity, but electricity can't be stored efficiently, so power plants using photovoltaic cells can't keep a city running 24 hours a day, 7 days a week.

We may not be able to store electricity, but storing the Sun's energy is sometimes an option. Scientists have developed ways of storing the heat energy collected by a CSP plant. The oil heated by the Sun's energy is used to heat up a type of salt. This salt is cheap and very efficient at storing heat. At night, it can transfer its heat back to the oil to keep the power station running.

STORING THE ENERGY

Batteries are a useful way of storing energy until it is needed. We can store solar energy in the same way, but the technology does not work very well. The batteries used for storing electricity produced by a home solar power setup are expensive and inefficient, and they often contain hazardous chemicals.

SOLAR POWER: THE COSTS

One of the reasons that solar power is still not widespread is the cost. In the past, electricity produced from solar power was much more expensive than electricity from other sources. This is because although sunshine is free, installing solar panels—either on a house or in a solar power plant—can be expensive. However, the price of solar panels is coming down, making solar power more affordable than it used to be.

Solar power plants need a lot of space for installing collectors and solar panels. They must also be built in places that get reliable sunshine, and not all locations are suitable. Even smaller home-based systems need regular sunshine to be worth the cost of installation. And a smaller house may not have the roof space to install as many solar panels as it needs.

Solar power can also have an impact on the environment. The manufacturing of solar panels often makes use of hazardous chemicals and can release gases that contribute to global warming. CSP plants need a lot of water for their cooling systems. Important habitats can be destroyed when solar power plants are built.

LARGE ARRAYS OF SOLAR PANELS MAY PREVENT FARMERS FROM GROWING CROPS ON THE LAND.

DUAL PURPOSE

Some solar panel designs allow farmers to graze sheep on the grass beneath them. The farmers can "farm" solar energy and livestock at the same time.

25

THE FUTURE

As we move away from fossil fuels, renewable energy sources will become even more important. There is so much potential in solar energy that it will certainly be a key player. However, when it comes to exploiting the Sun's energy, we are just getting started. Solar power currently makes up less than 1 percent of the world's electricity supply, but it is growing fast. Scientists predict that by 2050, photovoltaic and CSP plants will provide more than 10 percent of the world's electricity.

As the technology improves, the cost of manufacturing solar panels and collectors goes down, making solar energy more affordable. We will soon see more solar panels on rooftops, as well as in other locations such as parking lots, airports, and even on clothes and backpacks.

LEADING PRODUCERS
China, Germany, and Japan are the world's leading producers of solar energy. In 2015, China generated 43,500 megawatts from this source.

26

SOLAR-POWERED BACKPACKS CAN POWER A LAPTOP FOR UP TO THREE HOURS AND CHARGE CELL PHONES, CAMERAS, AND FLASHLIGHTS.

27

NEW TECHNOLOGIES

The list of machines that can be powered by solar energy is very long. We already use many devices with built-in solar panels, and in some places the electricity supply that we plug our chargers into is based on solar power.

Engineers are designing more and more machines that run on solar energy. There are solar cars, solar boats, and even solar airplanes. At the moment, most of these are not efficient enough to replace our current cars and commercial airliners, but that may change in the future.

Solar cells are getting smaller and more efficient. This means that less surface area is needed to produce electricity. You can already buy jackets with solar panels that charge your gadgets as you walk around. The possibilities are endless!

SPACE STATION

The International Space Station (ISS) is powered entirely by about 250,000 solar cells. Excess electricity generated during the day is stored for use during the night as the ISS orbits Earth.

THE PATHFINDER (BELOW) IS A REMOTELY PILOTED, SOLAR-POWERED AIRPLANE THAT CAN REMAIN AIRBORNE FOR UP TO 15 HOURS.

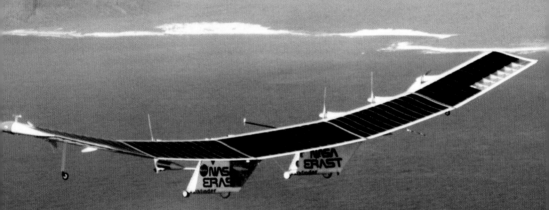

AROUND THE WORLD

The Solar Impulse 2 aircraft had its first flight in 2014. It became the first completely solar-powered plane to travel all the way around the world.

GLOSSARY

"carbon footprint": The amount of carbon dioxide given off by a person's activities.

conductors: Devices designed to transmit electricity.

electrodes: Conductors used to make contact with some part of an electrical circuit.

global warming: An increase in the average temperature of Earth's atmosphere.

grid: Power transmission network taking electricity from where it is generated to where it is needed.

infrared radiation: Radiation with a wavelength longer than visible light; it can be detected as heat.

megawatt (MW): A large unit of electricity. One MW can provide all the electricity for more than 150 houses.

nuclear reaction: A process that alters the energy level or composition of atomic nuclei.

pollution: The release of substances that have harmful or toxic effects into the atmosphere, rivers, or ocean.

power grid: A system of cables by which electrical power is distributed throughout a region.

semiconductor: A material that is neither a good conductor of electricity nor a good insulator; it has properties of electrical conductivity somewhere between the two.

toxic: Containing poisonous substances.

trillion: One million million (or one thousand billion).

ultraviolet radiation: Light with a wavelength shorter than visible light.

FURTHER INFORMATION

BOOKS

Bow, James. *Energy from the Sun*
(Next Generation Energy).
New York: Crabtree, 2015.

Challoner, Jack. *Energy* (Eyewitness).
New York: Dorling Kindersley, 2012.

Spetgang, Tilly. *The Kids' Solar Energy Book*.
Watertown, MA: Charlesbridge, 2011.

WEBSITES

Due to the changing nature of Internet links,
PowerKids Press has developed an online list
of websites related to the subject of this book.
This site is updated regularly. Please use this
link to access the list:

www.powerkidslinks.com/tfop/solar

INDEX